I0758077

Table of Contents

Everything You Need to Know About ADHD

What is ADHD?

Attention deficit hyperactivity disorder (ADHD) is a mental health disorder that can cause above-normal levels of hyperactive and impulsive behaviors. People with ADHD may also have trouble focusing their attention on a single task or sitting still for long periods of time.

Both adults and children can have ADHD. It's a diagnosis the American

Psychiatric Association (APA) recognizes.

ADHD symptoms

A wide range of behaviors are associated with ADHD. Some of the more common ones include:

- having trouble focusing or concentrating on tasks

- being forgetful about completing tasks

- being easily distracted

- having difficulty sitting still

- interrupting people while they're talking

If you or your child has ADHD, you may have some or all of these symptoms. The symptoms you have depend on the type of ADHD you have.

Types of ADHD

To make ADHD diagnoses more consistent, the APA has grouped the condition into three categories, or types. These types are predominantly inattentive, predominantly hyperactivity-impulsive, and a combination of both.

Predominantly inattentive

As the name suggests, people with this type of ADHD have extreme difficulty focusing, finishing tasks, and following instructions.

Experts also think that many children with the inattentive type of ADHD may not receive a proper diagnosis because they don't tend to disrupt the classroom. This type is most common among girls with ADHD.

Predominantly hyperactive-impulsive type

People with this type of ADHD show primarily hyperactive and impulsive behavior. This can include fidgeting, interrupting people while they're talking, and not being able to wait their turn.

Although inattention is less of a concern with this type of ADHD, people with predominantly hyperactive-impulsive ADHD may still find it difficult to focus on tasks.

Combined hyperactive-impulsive and inattentive type

This is the most common type of ADHD. People with this combined type of ADHD display both inattentive and hyperactive symptoms. These include an inability to pay attention, a tendency toward impulsiveness, and above-normal levels of activity and energy.

The type of ADHD you or your child has will determine how it's treated. The type you have can change over time, so your treatment may change, too.

ADD vs. ADHD

You may have heard the terms "ADD" and "ADHD" and wondered what the difference is between them.

ADD, or attention deficit disorder, is an outdated term. It was previously used to describe people who have problems paying attention but aren't hyperactive. The type of ADHD called predominantly inattentive is now used in place of ADD.

ADHD is the current overarching name of the condition. The term ADHD became official in May 2013, when the

APA released the Diagnostic and Statistical Manual of Mental Disorders, Fifth Edition (DSM-5).

This manual is what doctors refer to when making diagnoses for mental health conditions.

Adult ADHD

More than 60 percent of children with ADHD still exhibit symptoms as adults. But for many people, ADHD symptoms decrease or become less frequent as they get older.

That said, treatment is important. Untreated ADHD in adults can have a negative impact on many aspects of life. Symptoms such as trouble managing time, forgetfulness, and impatience can cause problems at work, home, and in all types of relationships.

ADHD in children

One in 10 children between ages 5 to 17 years receives an ADHD diagnosis, making this one of the most common childhood neurodevelopmental disorders in the United States.

For children, ADHD is generally associated with problems at school.

Children with ADHD often have trouble succeeding in a controlled classroom setting.

Boys are more than twice as likely as girls to receive an ADHD diagnosis. This may be because boys tend to exhibit hallmark symptoms of hyperactivity. Although some girls with ADHD may have the classic symptoms of hyperactivity, many don't. In many cases, girls with ADHD may:

• daydream frequently

• be hyper-talkative rather than hyperactive

Many symptoms of ADHD can be typical childhood behaviors, so it can be hard to know what's ADHD-related and what's not.

What causes ADHD?

Despite how common ADHD is, doctors and researchers still aren't sure what causes the condition. It's believed to have neurological origins. Genetics may also play a role.

Research suggests that a reduction in dopamine is a factor in ADHD. Dopamine is a chemical in the brain that helps move signals from one nerve to another. It plays a role in triggering emotional responses and movements.

Other research suggests a structural difference in the brain. Findings indicate that people with ADHD have less gray matter volume. Gray matter includes the brain areas that help with:

- speech

- self-control

- decision-making

- muscle control

Researchers are still studying potential causes of ADHD, such as smoking during pregnancy.

ADHD testing and diagnosis

There's no single test that can tell if you or your child has ADHD. A recent study highlighted the benefits of a new test to diagnose adult ADHD, but many clinicians believe an ADHD diagnosis can't be made based on one test.

To make a diagnosis, your doctor will assess any symptoms you or your child has had over the previous six months.

Your doctor will likely gather information from teachers or family members and may use checklists and rating scales to review symptoms. They'll also do a physical exam to check for other health problems.

If you suspect that you or your child has ADHD, talk to your doctor about getting an evaluation. For your child, you can also talk to their school counselor. Schools regularly assess children for problems that may be affecting their educational performance.

For the assessment, provide your doctor or counselor with notes and observations about you or your child's behavior.

If they suspect ADHD, they may refer you or your child to an ADHD specialist. Depending on the diagnosis, they may also suggest making an appointment with a psychiatrist or neurologist.

ADHD treatment

Treatment for ADHD typically includes behavioral therapies, medication, or both.

Types of therapy include psychotherapy, or talk therapy. With talk therapy, you or your child will discuss how ADHD affects your life and ways to help you manage it.

Another therapy type is behavioral therapy. This therapy can help you or your child with learning how to monitor and manage your behavior.

Medication can also be very helpful when you're living with ADHD. ADHD medications are designed to affect brain chemicals in a way that enables you to better control your impulses and actions.

ADHD medication

The two main types of medications used to treat ADHD are stimulants and nonstimulants.

Central nervous system (CNS) stimulants are the most commonly prescribed ADHD medications. These drugs work by increasing the amounts of the brain chemicals dopamine and norepinephrine.

Examples of these drugs include methylphenidate (Ritalin) and amphetamine-based stimulants (Adderall).

If stimulants don't work well for you or your child, or if they cause troublesome side effects, your doctor may suggest a nonstimulant medication. Certain nonstimulant medications work by increasing levels of norepinephrine in the brain.

These medications include atomoxetine (Strattera) and some antidepressants such as bupropion (Wellbutrin).

ADHD medications can have many benefits, as well as side effects.

Natural remedies for ADHD

In addition to — or instead of — medication, several remedies have been suggested to help improve ADHD symptoms.

For starters, following a healthy lifestyle may help you or your child manage ADHD symptoms. The Centers for Disease Control and Prevention (CDC) recommends the following:

- eat a healthy, balanced diet

• get at least 60 minutes of physical activity per day

• get plenty of sleep

• limit daily screen time from phones, computers, and TV

Studies have also shown that yoga, tai chi, and spending time outdoors can help calm overactive minds and may ease ADHD symptoms.

Mindfulness meditation is another option. Research in adults and teens has shown meditation to have positive effects on attention and thought processes, as well as on anxiety and depression.

Avoiding certain allergens and food additives are also potential ways to help reduce ADHD symptoms.

Is ADHD a disability?

While ADHD is a neurodevelopmental disorder, it's not considered a learning disability. However, ADHD symptoms can make it harder for you to learn. Also, it's possible for ADHD to occur in some individuals who also have learning disabilities.

To help relieve any impact on learning for children, teachers can map out individual guidelines for a student with ADHD. This may include allowing extra time for assignments and tests or developing a personal reward system.

Although it's not technically a disability, ADHD can have lifelong effects.

ADHD and depression

If you or your child has ADHD, you're more likely to have depression as well. In fact, the rate of major depression in children with ADHD is more than five times higher than in children without ADHD. Up to 31 percent of adults with ADHD have been found to also have depression.

This may feel like an unfair double whammy, but know that treatments are available for both conditions. The treatments often overlap. Talk therapy can help treat both conditions. Also, certain antidepressants, such as bupropion, can sometimes help ease ADHD symptoms.

Of course, having ADHD doesn't guarantee that you'll have depression, but it's important to know it's a possibility.

Tips for coping with ADHD

If you or your child has ADHD, a consistent schedule with structure and regular expectations may be helpful. For adults, using lists, keeping a calendar, and setting reminders are good ways to help you get and stay organized. For children, it can be helpful to focus on writing down homework assignments and keeping everyday items, such as toys and backpacks, in assigned spots.

Learning more about the disorder in general can also help you learn how to manage it. Organizations like Children and Adults with Attention Deficit Disorder or the Attention Deficit Disorder Association provide tips for management as well as the latest research.

Your doctor can provide more guidance in ways to manage your ADHD symptoms.

Outlook

For children and adults, untreated ADHD can have a serious impact on your life. It can affect school, work, and relationships. Treatment is important to lessen the effects of the condition.

But it's still important to keep in mind that many people with ADHD enjoy fulfilling and successful lives. Some even tout the benefits of the condition.

If you think you or your child may have ADHD, your first step should be talking to your doctor. They can help determine if ADHD is a factor for you or your child. Your doctor can help you create a treatment plan to help you manage your symptoms and live well with ADHD.

14 Signs of Attention Deficit Hyperactivity Disorder (ADHD)

Attention deficit hyperactivity disorder (ADHD) is a complex neurodevelopmental disorder that can affect a child's success at school, as well as their relationships. The symptoms of ADHD vary and are sometimes difficult to recognize.

Any child may experience many of the individual symptoms of ADHD. So, to make a diagnosis, your child's doctor will need to evaluate your child using several criteria.

ADHD is generally diagnosed in children by the time they're teenagers, with the average age for moderate ADHD diagnosis being 7 years old.

Older children exhibiting symptoms may have ADHD, but they've often exhibited rather elaborate symptoms early in life.

For information about ADHD symptoms in adults, this article can help.

Here are 14 common signs of ADHD in children:

1. Self-focused behavior

A common sign of ADHD is what looks like an inability to recognize other people's needs and desires. This can lead to the next two signs:

• interrupting

• trouble waiting their turn

2. Interrupting

Self-focused behavior may cause a child with ADHD to interrupt others while they're talking or butt into conversations or games they're not part of.

3. Trouble waiting their turn

Kids with ADHD may have trouble waiting their turn during classroom activities or when playing games with other children.

4. Emotional turmoil

A child with ADHD may have trouble keeping their emotions in check. They may have outbursts of anger at inappropriate times.

Younger children may have temper tantrums.

5. Fidgeting

Children with ADHD often can't sit still. They may try to get up and run around, fidget, or squirm in their chair when forced to sit.

6. Problems playing quietly

Fidgetiness can make it difficult for kids with ADHD to play quietly or engage calmly in leisure activities.

7. Unfinished tasks

A child with ADHD may show interest in lots of different things, but they may have problems finishing them. For example, they may start projects, chores, or homework, but move on to the next thing that catches their interest before finishing.

8. Lack of focus

A child with ADHD may have trouble paying attention — even when someone is speaking directly to them.

They'll say they heard you, but they won't be able to repeat back what you just said.

9. Avoidance of tasks needing extended mental effort

This same lack of focus can cause a child to avoid activities that require a sustained mental effort, such as paying attention in class or doing homework.

10. Mistakes

Children with ADHD may have trouble following instructions that require planning or executing a plan. This can then lead to careless mistakes — but it doesn't indicate laziness or a lack of intelligence.

11. Daydreaming

Children with ADHD aren't always rambunctious and loud. Another sign of ADHD is being quieter and less involved than other kids.

A child with ADHD may stare into space, daydream, and ignore what's going on around them.

12. Trouble getting organized

A child with ADHD may have trouble keeping track of tasks and activities. This can cause problems at school, as they can find it hard to prioritize homework, school projects, and other assignments.

13. Forgetfulness

Kids with ADHD may be forgetful in daily activities. They may forget to do chores or their homework. They may also lose things often, such as toys.

14. Symptoms in multiple settings

A child with ADHD will show symptoms of the condition in more than one setting. For instance, they may show lack of focus both in school and at home.

Symptoms as children get older

As children with ADHD get older, they'll oftentimes not have as much self-control as other children their own age. This can make kids and adolescents with ADHD seem immature compared to their peers.

Some daily tasks that adolescents with ADHD may have trouble with include:

- focusing on schoolwork and assignments

- reading social cues

- compromising with peers

- maintaining personal hygiene

- helping out with chores at home

- time management

- driving safely

Looking forward

All children are going to exhibit some of these behaviors at some point. Daydreaming, fidgeting, and persistent interruptions are all common behaviors in children.

You should start thinking about the next steps if:

- your child regularly displays signs of ADHD

- this behavior is affecting their success in school and leading to negative interactions with peers

ADHD is treatable. If your child is diagnosed with ADHD, review all of the treatment options. Then, set up a time to meet with a doctor or psychologist to determine the best course of action.

7 Ways to Calm Your Child with ADHD

To help your child thrive, highlight the positives. Here's how you can create healthy habits.

All children are different, and it's these differences that make them unique and fascinating. As parents, our mission is to nurture these distinctive traits and help our children achieve all the things they put their minds to.

To help them thrive, we generally highlight their positives while downplaying the negatives. The problems arise when we see these remarkable differences as deficits.

A child's hyperactivity may seem like a negative. And while hyperactivity and other symptoms of attention deficit hyperactivity disorder (ADHD) can stand in the way of productivity and attention, they're part of that child and, if managed, can also allow them to grow and thrive.

So, what are the best ways to calm your child with ADHD and help them obtain success?

1. Follow instructions

If your child is diagnosed with ADHD and begins treatment, as a parent, it's your job to follow through on recommendations.

If you decide that medication for your child is best for the both of you, consistency is critical. It's important to know that it's difficult to tell if your child's treatment is working when done sporadically. It's also important to communicate with their doctor if you have concerns about medication selection and side effects.

During this time, it's important to seek other services like parent training, social skills groups, and therapy for your child to help improve their symptoms.

2. Be consistent with your parenting

Just like you need to be consistent with treatment instructions, you need to be consistent at home. Children with ADHD succeed in environments that are consistent. This means that there must be a sense of structure and routine at home.

You may notice that hyperactivity becomes worse during unstructured times — and without supervision, hyperactivity may increase to an excessive level. By building a routine with some flexibility, you create fewer possibilities for hyperactivity to intensify.

Over time, a stable structure can transform into healthy practices. This will provide your child with the ability to manage their hyperactivity. While you don't need to micromanage, you do need to put some reasonable orderliness into place.

3. Break up homework with activities

Asking a person with ADHD to sit still and stay quiet for a certain amount of time is insensitive. It's better to break up activities that require calmness into chunks of time to help them succeed.

If your child can only tolerate a few minutes of homework, ask them to do as much as they can in those minutes. Following the work, they can take a three-minute break to stretch, hop around, or whatever they decide on before they sit down for another couple of minutes.

This approach ensures that their time sitting down is productive versus being filled with squirming and excessive movements.

4. Form the behavior

Shaping is a psychological method used in behavioral and cognitive behavioral therapies. In shaping, you accept the behavior at its baseline and work to make small changes with the use of reinforcement.

If you wanted to incorporate shaping into the previous homework example, you would start at six minutes, break, seven minutes, break, eight minutes, until their homework is complete.

When your child accomplishes the fixed amount of time at regular activity levels, you give a reward. Rewards can be kind words, a hug, small amounts of money, or a fun activity later on. This process empowers your child to associate extended periods of desired activity levels with positives. With consistency, the times will stretch and become longer.

5. Allow them to fidget

Allow your child to fidget while engaging in a task that requires a lot of patience. Allowing them to play with a small toy, a piece of clothing, or a fidget tool (like a fidget cube) can help improve attention and focus while simultaneously reducing activity levels.

6. Let your child play before taking on big tasks

Your child may do well if they're allowed to burn off excess energy through playtime before they're expected to sit still for a number of minutes.

For example, if your child has been sitting all day and bottling up their energy, completing homework as soon as they arrive home may not be the answer. Instead, find some physically-demanding, fun activities for them to do when they first get home.

Allowing your child to play for a half hour may make focusing on homework more effective and efficient.

7. Help them practice relaxation

Learning about, practicing, and teaching your child about relaxation techniques may help to increase their awareness and understanding of their bodies, feelings, behaviors, and hyperactivity.

These can include deep breathing exercises, progressive muscle relaxation, mindfulness meditation, visualization, and yoga. There are more relaxation techniques out there as well!

Finding the best times to implement these skills will take some experimentation, but the results will be worth it.

ADHD Treatment Options

ADHD is a disorder that affects the brain and behaviors. There's no known cure for ADHD, but several options can help your child manage their symptoms.

Treatments range from behavioral intervention to prescription medication. In many cases, medication alone is an effective treatment for ADHD. However, the National Institute of Mental Health suggests that including other options is important. Read on to learn about the options available today for treating ADHD.

Stimulant and nonstimulant medications

Medication is often an important part of treatment for a child with ADHD. However, it can be a difficult decision to make as a parent.

To make the best choice, you and your child's doctor should work together to decide if medication is a good option. If so, ask the doctor whether your child needs medication during school hours only, or on evenings and weekends as well. You and the doctor should also determine what type of medication might be best. The two main types of ADHD medications are stimulants and nonstimulants.

Central nervous system stimulants

Central nervous system (CNS) stimulants are the most commonly prescribed class of ADHD drugs. These drugs work by increasing the amounts of the brain chemicals called dopamine and norepinephrine. The effect improves your child's concentration and helps them focus better.

Common CNS stimulants used to treat ADHD include:

- amphetamine-based stimulants (Adderall, Dexedrine, Dextrostat)

- dextromethamphetamine (Desoxyn)

- dextromethylphenidate (Focalin)

- methylphenidate (Concerta, Daytrana, Metadate, Ritalin)

Non-stimulant medications

Your child's doctor may consider nonstimulant medications when stimulants haven't worked or have caused side effects that your child finds hard to handle.

Certain nonstimulant medications work by increasing levels of norepinephrine in your child's brain. Norepinephrine is thought to help with attention and memory. These nonstimulant treatments include:

• atomoxetine (Strattera)

• antidepressants like nortriptyline (Pamelor)

Other nonstimulant medications can also help with ADHD. It isn't fully known how these medications help with ADHD, but there is some evidence that they help certain chemicals work better in the part of the brain involved with attention and memory. These other nonstimulants include:

• guanfacine (Intuniv)

• clonidine (Kapvay)

Side effects of stimulants and non-stimulants

The more common side effects of stimulants and nonstimulants are pretty similar, although they tend to be stronger for stimulants. These side effects can include:

- headache

- trouble sleeping

- stomach upset

- nervousness

- irritability

- weight loss

- dry mouth

The more serious side effects of these drug types are rarer. For stimulants, the serious side effects in children can include:

- hallucinations (seeing or hearing things that aren't there)

- increased blood pressure

- allergic reaction

- suicidal thoughts or actions

For nonstimulants, the serious side effects in children can include:

- seizures

- suicidal thoughts or actions

Therapeutic ADHD treatments

Several therapy options can help children with ADHD. Talk to your doctor about whether one or more of these options would be a good choice for your child.

Psychotherapy

Psychotherapy can be useful in getting your child to open up about their feelings of coping with ADHD. ADHD can cause your child to have problems with peers and authority figures. Psychotherapy can help children better handle these relationships.

In psychotherapy, a child may also be able to explore their behavior patterns and learn how to make good choices in the future. And family therapy can be a great way to help figure out how best to work through disruptive behaviors.

Behavior therapy

The goal of behavior therapy (BT) is to teach a child how to monitor their behaviors and then change those behaviors appropriately. You and your child, and perhaps the child's teacher, will work together. You'll develop strategies for how your child behaves in response to certain situations. These strategies often involve some sort of direct feedback to help the child learn suitable behaviors. For instance, a token reward system could be devised to support positive behaviors.

Social skills training

Social skills training can sometimes be useful if a child shows serious issues dealing with social environments. As with BT, the goal of social skills training is to teach the child new and more appropriate behaviors. This helps a child with ADHD play and work better with others. A therapist may try to teach behaviors such as:

- waiting their turn

- sharing toys

- asking for help

- dealing with teasing

Support groups

Support groups are great for helping parents of children with ADHD connect with others who may share similar experiences and concerns. Support groups typically meet regularly to allow relationships and support networks to be built. Knowing you're not alone in dealing with ADHD can be a huge relief for many parents.

Support groups can also be a great resource for ideas and strategies for coping with your child's ADHD, especially if your child was recently diagnosed. Ask your doctor how to find support groups in your area.

Parenting skills training

Parenting skills training gives you tools and techniques for understanding and managing your child's behaviors. Some techniques may include the following:

Immediate rewards: Try using a point system or other means of immediate rewards for good behavior or work.

Timeouts: Use a timeout when your child becomes too unruly or out of control. For some children, being pulled out of a stressful or overstimulating situation can help them learn how to react more appropriately the next time a similar situation comes up.

Togetherness: Find time together every week to share a pleasurable or relaxing activity. During this time together, you can look for opportunities to point out what your child does well and praise their strengths and abilities.

Striving for success: Structure situations in a way that allows your child to find success. For instance, you might allow them to have only one or two playmates at a time so they don't get overstimulated.

Stress management: Use methods such as meditation, relaxation techniques, and exercise to help manage stress.

Behavioral interventions for home and school

One of the biggest concerns for parents of children with ADHD is their child's success in school. A lot of that success depends on how organized they are. Being organized is a skill that many children with ADHD struggle with. Simple steps such as these below can be an immense help.

Build a schedule

Set the same routine every day. Try to make sure that waking up, bedtime, homework, and even playtime are done at consistent times. Post the schedule in a visible place. If a change must be made, make it as far in advance as possible.

Organize everyday items

Make sure that clothing, backpacks, school supplies, and play items all have a designated, clearly marked space.

Use homework and notebook organizers

Stress the importance of writing down assignments and bringing home anything needed to complete homework.

Ask about using a computer in class

For some children with ADHD, handwriting is another obstacle to success. If necessary, see if their teacher will allow for computer use in the classroom.

Use positive reinforcement

Children with ADHD often receive criticism from authority figures. Then they start to expect it. If they get only negative feedback without ever hearing positive things about themselves, they'll start to think of themselves as bad.

To boost your child's self-esteem and reinforce appropriate behavior, use positive reinforcement. If your child follows the rules and behaves well, give small rewards and praise. This lets them know what behavior you prefer, while letting them know that they can be good.

Talk with your doctor

Effective treatment for a child's ADHD often includes several approaches. These can include medication and one or more types of therapy, as well as behavioral measures that you can put into practice as a parent. Getting proper treatment can help your child manage their ADHD symptoms and feel better about themselves.

How ADHD Changes in Teens

Adolescence sparks so many physical, mental, and emotional changes that you might wonder whether ADHD also changes during your teen years. The answer is yes... and no.

ADHD doesn't disappear when people enter adolescence. Some symptoms might settle down, but others might flare up. If your symptoms change and new challenges emerge, it's important to know what to do about them, whether you're a young adult with ADHD or the parent of one.

Here's what to know about how ADHD affects adolescents.

What is ADHD?

Attention deficit hyperactivity disorder (ADHD) is a health condition that makes it harder for people to:

• pay attention for long periods of time

• organize and follow through on complex tasks

• focus in the presence of distraction

• control impulses

- remain still and quiet

These symptoms may interfere with your ability to function at home, in social settings, and at school or work.

It's important to note that in childhood, the teen years, and adulthood, ADHD can look different from person to person. Cultural factors, sex and gender, and individual personalities can all shape how ADHD presents. This can make it harder to recognize, diagnose, and treat.

What is ADHD like for teens?

ADHD is not only a childhood condition. Researchers say roughly 60 percent of people diagnosed with ADHD in childhood will continue experiencing symptoms into adulthood.

That means along with all the other changes adolescence brings, you might also notice some changes in how your ADHD presents. Here are some examples of how ADHD may affect you during your teen years:

Changes in hyperactivity

Many people's symptoms improve during adolescence. Which symptoms continue and which ones abate can vary from person to person.

One of the hallmarks of childhood ADHD is high energy and an inability to sit still. The amount of physical movement might change for some teens with ADHD. For example, hyperactivity may morph into general restlessness, but inattention and impulsivity may persist.

Academic ups and downs

In late middle school and high school, academic demands increase at the same time as parents and teachers begin expecting students to show more self-discipline and independence. A variety of circumstances can lead to academic challenges:

• The practicalities of high school — changing classrooms, having different teachers, and using lockers — can make it harder to stay organized.

• An increasing number of complex or long-term academic projects can tax your time management skills.

• Collaborating with other students can be a challenge if socializing is difficult for you.

• Fewer parental and educational supports coupled with more independence and autonomy could lead to a drop in academic performance.

Relationship conflicts

For some people with ADHD, social conflicts can intensify or increase during this period. Social conflict isn't uncommon among teens, but ADHD may present added challenges.

Studies show that some people with ADHD may have a harder time socializing than others. Engaging in extracurricular activities and having parents who are involved, attentive, and positive can help make socializing easier for people with ADHD.

Research also shows that conflicts between children and parents or guardians, along with conflicts in romantic relationships, might arise.

There may be a tendency among some parents of adolescents with ADHD to become overly protective — possibly even controlling. Attentive and caring parenting styles usually feel more supportive.

While social conflicts in friendships, families, and dating relationships aren't uncommon in teen years, they may be more of an issue if you have ADHD.

Mood and self-esteem differences

ADHD symptoms may make normal fluctuations in mood and self-esteem more extreme. Some people with ADHD feel particularly irritable during their teen years. Studies show that more authoritarian and less egalitarian parenting styles may make irritability worse.

If you are having trouble in school or in important relationships, you might also be feeling more stress or anxiety than you are used to feeling.

Research shows that, for some teens with ADHD, anger can trigger substance use. Stress, poor sleep habits, emerging mood disorders, and substance use can make it harder to pinpoint what's causing changes to mood and self-esteem.

Parenting toolkit: Training may help

Parents, if you sometimes find it stressful parenting a teen with ADHD, you're not alone. Seeking some extra training could make a big difference. Research shows that mindfulness and emotional intelligence training can improve both your parent-child relationship and developmental outcomes for your teen.

Sleep pattern changes

During adolescence, lots of physiological changes can affect sleep patterns:

• Hormones can change your circadian rhythms (the internal "clock" that sets your sleep/wake cycle).

• Sleep spindles and other brain structures that regulate sleep are maturing.

• School demands and social activities may also disrupt your usual sleep schedule.

While these changes are normal, they may complicate matters for people with ADHD, since 25–55 percent of young people with ADHD already have trouble getting good sleep. People who take stimulant medications to treat ADHD may take longer to fall asleep, wake up more often at night, or not sleep as well overall.

Escalation in risk-taking

When teens with ADHD get behind the wheel, impulsivity may cause accidents. Studies show that ADHD is associated with a higher number of car accidents — an average of one accident every 2 years.

Sexual maturity can also involve some potentially dangerous risk-taking. Risky sexual behaviors tend to be more common if you use cannabis or have a conduct disorder at the same time.

Substance use could become problematic. A small 2018 study found that adolescents who had more severe ADHD symptoms in childhood had a greater risk of substance use. The study also found that people whose dominant symptom was inattention gravitated toward cannabis use, while those with impulsivity and hyperactivity symptoms used both cannabis and alcohol, often in binge patterns.

The bright side

Though adolescence presents new challenges for people with ADHD, it also affords new opportunities.

As academic studies become more difficult, problems with organization and attention may become more obvious, which means some teens are able to get a more accurate diagnosis and receive an effective treatment plan for the first time.

Along with the struggles faced by teens with ADHD, there may also be traits that are considered positive, like creativity, high energy levels, and for some, the ability to hyperfocus on specific tasks.

There are also indications that, during adolescence, the cerebral cortex in the brain may develop new connections, helping some teens learn new ways to compensate for their ADHD symptoms.

As teens mature, they may be able to articulate their symptoms more clearly, helping parents, educators, and healthcare providers better meet their needs and making them more effective self-advocates.

Why do people get ADHD?

Researchers aren't sure exactly what causes ADHD. There appears to be a genetic connection: If you have a sibling with ADHD, for example, you're roughly twice as likely to have the disorder yourself.

There also seem to be some structural differences in parts of the brain that control impulses, researchers say. While impulse control can be a challenge for any teen, differences in the way the brain develops may make the problem more likely in teens with ADHD.

What are common risk factors for developing ADHD?

Research shows that people whose ADHD symptoms are severe are more likely to have ADHD that persists into the teen years. ADHD also tends to continue into the teen years for people who also have conduct and depression disorders.

Some common risk factors for ADHD include:

- having a parent who smoked cigarettes or used alcohol during pregnancy

- having a parent who was exposed to lead or other environmental toxins while pregnant

- having a low birth weight

- experiencing a brain injury

Parenting toolkit: Strategies research supports

Researchers analyzed the parenting methods that produced healthier outcomes among children and adolescents with ADHD. Healthy behaviors in the child were associated with positive parenting practices, such as rules, routines, caregiving, and positive stimulation. ADHD symptoms and behaviors were typically worse when parents used excessive physical punishments and yelling.